Jungian Typology

Jungian Typology

Myers Briggs and Personality

Dr Stephen Moss

Collins Dove
Melbourne Australia

This book is a commentary on Jung's Type Theory.
It does not purport to be the Myers Briggs Type Indicator.
MBTI is a registered trade mark of Consulting Psychologists
Press Inc., 577 College Av., Palo Alto, Ca, 94306, USA.

Published by Collins Dove
60–64 Railway Road,
Blackburn, Victoria 3130
Telephone (03) 877 1333

First published 1989

Designed by Jo Brazil
Cover design by Jo Brazil
Typeset in 14pt Times by Collins Dove Desktop
Printed in Australia by The Book Printer

The National Library of Australia
Cataloguing-in-Publication Data:

Moss, Stephen, Dr.
    Jungian typology: Myers Briggs and personality.
    ISBN 0 85924 771 6.

    1. Myers-Briggs Type Indicator. 2. Typology
    (Psychology), 3. Personality tests.
    4. Self-evaluation. I. Title.

155.2'64

Contents

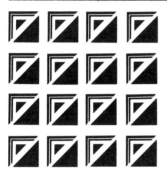

Introduction

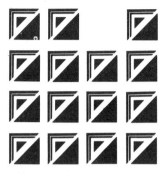

This handbook was designed and written to be used in conjunction with the Myers Briggs Type Indicator (MBTI). It can be used as a training aid or as a stand-alone text on Jungian type theory. If you have not already done so it is recommended that you complete an MBTI questionnaire. You can then use this handbook to better understand your results and their practical application to life and work.

It is commonly accepted that people are different. Jungian type theory explains some of these basic differences or preferences, and encourages the genuine valuing of those differences. An understanding of type in general and your own type in particular can lead to better problem solving, conflict resolution, increased

1

self-understanding; it can help you choose or adjust your career and it can, in a very practical way, help you on the job. This handbook offers a number of ways for you to explore your own preferences and verify your own type.

Jung's Type Theory reports your type by four letters that indicate where you come out on each of the four preferences: Extravert–Introvert (E–I); Sensing–Intuition (S–N); Thinking–Feeling (T–F); and Judging–Perceiving (J–P). The sixteen possible combinations of these four dimensions are called type profiles

Use this handbook to assist your understanding and practical use of psychological type theory. Remember that we are all unique human beings and type theory is only meant to help understand some of the basic differences between people. The theory does not sum up all human behaviour and should be used to simply verify one's own observation and experience.

The Theory

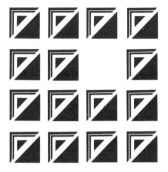

Carl Jung in his 1921 publication *Psychological Types* (Collected Works volume 6) elaborated a complex and yet profoundly insightful theory of personality. Jung called the study the 'fruit of nearly twenty years work in the domain of practical psychology'.

In a nutshell, Jung's *Psychological Types* explains that apparently random behaviour in fact has a distinct pattern and order to it. People are born with fundamental tendencies and preferences of personality—these he called 'types'.

Jung defined four basic mental functions or processes common to all people. Two of these functions are concerned with how people take in information; these he called the Perceiving functions of Sensation and Intuition. All of us have a preference for one of these two ways of taking in information. The other two functions are related to how people make decisions; these he called the Judging functions of Thinking and Feeling. We also have a preference for one of these two functions.

In order to develop a strong personality and ego we tend to specialise in two of these functions—one from each pair—and neglect the other two functions. We still have all four functions but there tends to be a pattern in our use of these functions. This is what determines our 'type'.

To understand this concept of preference it is helpful to use the analogy of right or left handedness. If you try writing your name with your less preferred hand it is more awkward, uncomfortable and less natural. To write with your preferred hand comes more naturally; you don't have to think about it and you feel more comfortable. Using your preferred functions in life is like using your preferred hand. Using your less preferred functions is like using your less preferred hand.

All of us use all our preferences or functions at different times, but not all at once and not, in most cases, with equal confidence and ability.

4

When asked to choose, therefore, most people can and do indicate a preference.

Additionally, each of these functions of our psychology can be either Extraverted or Introverted. Again, we are all capable of both Extravert and Introvert behaviour. It is simply that there is a natural tendency in us for one over the other.

The Myers Briggs Type Indicator (MBTI)

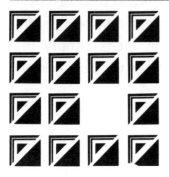

Isabel Myers and Katherine Briggs, daughter and mother, set about developing the MBTI* from Jung's *Psychological Types* from the 1940s in the United States. They wanted to make this remarkable theory usable and accessible to ordinary people. Before Isabel Myers' death in 1980, she witnessed the MBTI's publication in some sixteen languages and its development as one of the best-selling psychological tests in the world.

The MBTI is a self-report forced choice questionnaire. The present form (Form G) has 126 questions or items which a respondent completes by choosing one answer over another for each item. This is hand or computer scored by a psychologist or qualified MBTI admin-

* MBTI is a registered trademark of Consulting Psychologists Press Inc.

6

istrator and reported on an MBTI report form.

The MBTI measures your preference on four separate scales:

E Extravert–Introvert I
S Sensation–Intuition N
T Thinking–Feeling F
J Judging–Perceiving P

and delivers a 'type' by showing your preference on each scale, e.g. INTP, ESFP, ISTJ and so on.

The MBTI differs from Jung's theory in that it scientifically measures what Jung said were fundamental but basically unmeasurable preferences of personality. Jung also did not isolate the Extravert and Introvert attitudes from the functions or the Judging and Perceiving scale. The MBTI, however, has enabled people to find their type fairly easily. As with any psychological test, the MBTI has limitations, but it is usually remarkably accurate and therefore can be very useful.

What follows now are definitions of the preferences as Jung's Type Theory sets them out.

Extravert–Introvert

Australian population E = 40%, I = 60%
US population E = 55%, I = 45%

Where do you prefer to focus your attention?

This scale describes two ways of focusing attention on the outer and inner world.

Extraverts

People who prefer Extraversion tend to focus on the outer world of people and things. When people are using their Extravert function they are energised and stimulated by the outer world. Extraverts will probably appear to be more:

Active
Spontaneous
Relaxed
Enthusiastic
'Other' oriented
Liking variety

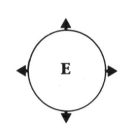

Introverts

People who prefer Introversion tend to focus more on their inner world of ideas. When people are using their Introvert function they are energised and stimulated by what goes on in their minds. Introverts will probably appear to be more:

Reserved
Passive
Quiet
Intense
Reflective
Doing one thing at a time

Think of some examples—the following are only generalisations, but they may help:

Extraverts enjoy small talk, Introverts say 'why talk when there is nothing to say?'.

When Extraverts are sick or tired they will tend to get stimulated and feel a little better by having people around; for Introverts it is quite the opposite.

Extraverts can talk to a whole group of people at once, whereas Introverts would prefer to talk to one person fairly intensely.

When an Extravert and an Introvert have a quarrel, the Extravert will tend to let off steam and it will all be finished; the Introvert may well say months later 'Do you remember when you said "such and such" three months ago?'.

An Extravert needs to live life in order to understand it, and an Introvert needs to understand life in order to live it.

Introverts tend to have a need for more social space than Extraverts. For example, Extraverts will stand closer when they talk to each other than will Introverts.

Extraverts find it easier to 'pull up their roots' and move about, both in their work and in their home life. Introverts tend to put down deeper roots; for example, they tend to stay in jobs longer than do Extraverts.

Introverts tend to be pessimistic and cautious, whereas Extraverts tend to be more confident and optimistic.

Using these statements and other examples you can think of within these definitions you can now plot your type on the scale below.

MY LIFE ORIENTATION

E|_____|_____|I
EXTRAVERTED   INTROVERTED

Sensing–Intuition

Australian and US population S = 75%, N = 25%

How do you acquire information?
This scale describes two mutually exclusive ways of finding things out. These we call the two Perceiving functions.

Sensing
People who have a developed Sensing function will tend to use their eyes, ears and other senses to tell them what is there and actually happening. Sensing is therefore especially useful for appreciating the realities of the situation. Sensing types tend to be realistic and practical, down to earth and aware of what is going on in the

here and now. They like to use what is known and proven.
Earthy
Realistic
Practical
Observant
Steady paced

Intuitive
People who have a developed Intuitive function will tend to take in information indirectly. Although initially information is received through the five senses, it is blurred and taken into the unconscious as it were, and linked with ideas and associations. Intuitive types tend therefore to be good with theories and hunches; they can see patterns in complexity and are very good in the overall planning stage of a project where there are few precedents to use.
Idealistic
Creative
Over-committed
Looking for meaning
Imaginative

In growing up, then, we tend to trust one of these two ways of perceiving. For one function to be well developed the other must be neglected and left out for a time. One is more focused and

11

has our energy and attention as it were. The following examples may help you to decide which is your preference:

Sensates tend to prefer factual books; Intuitives prefer fantasy and science fiction.

Intuitives often misplace their car keys, Sensates seldom do.

If there is a policy or instruction manual a Sensate will use it and an Intuitive will tend to ignore it.

In taking and giving directions, Sensates will tend to be detailed and exact, whereas Intuitives may give hazy generalisations.

Five Sensates seeing the one incident, such as a motor accident, will report the same things. Five Intuitives seeing the same motor accident will probably tell five or even more stories of what happened and how.

Intuitives tend to work in bursts of energy whereas Sensates are steady paced and practical.

Sensates may have a morning ritual, doing the same things the same way every day, whereas Intuitives can be quite random in this regard.

In conversation Sensates will use facts and details whereas Intuitives will tend to be more abstract, using metaphors, symbols and generalisations.

For the Intuitive the idea or the vision is more important and interesting than the reality; for the Sensate the reality is valued most highly.

Intuitives will question the meaning of things, whereas Sensates tend to take words at their face value.

Sensing types tend to pace themselves in a job, whereas Intuitives often get over-committed.

Using these statements and other examples you can think of within these definitions you can now plot your type on the scale below.

HOW DO I FIND THINGS OUT?

S|_____|_____|N
FIVE SENSES   SIXTH SENSE

Thinking–Feeling

Australian and US population T = 50%, F = 50%

How do you make your decisions?

This scale describes the two opposite or mutually exclusive styles of judging, i.e. coming to conclusions or making decisions. This dimension is concerned with the priorities we consider during the decision-making process.

13

Thinking

One way to decide is through your Thinking function. People with a highly developed Thinking function will first want to be logical, orderly and systematic. They give priority to deciding things objectively on the basis of cause and effect. This is not to say they exclude their feelings but their feelings are usually kept in some order during the decision process. People with a preference for Thinking seek an objective standard of truth and are frequently good at analysing people and situations objectively.

Firm
Exact
Fair
Argumentative
Blunt
Deliberate

Feeling

The other way to decide is through your Feeling function. People with a highly developed Feeling function will first want to consult their own value system in making a decision—what is important, valuable and meaningful for them. Again, this is not to the exclusion of the objective Thinking function but a priority for making decisions from what they believe in and what they consider important. Those with a

14

preference for Feeling tend to seek harmony in relationships and tend to deal with people tactfully and with apparently more care than the Thinking type.

Flexible
Heart driven
Need harmony
Relaxed
Subtle
Agreeable

It is important to note in this dimension that Thinking and Feeling types can be equally intelligent and equally emotional. This dimension is speaking about the priority we place in making a decision, so the word 'feeling' in this context means making decisions based on values.

Some examples, again generalisations, will serve to further explain the difference between the types:

Thinking types want to be respected whereas Feeling types want to be liked.

Thinking types can hurt people unintentionally; Feeling types will know they have hurt somebody.

Feeling types like to help people... Thinking types don't like to be helped!

In an argument over an issue a Thinking type

is more likely to stick more closely to the logic of the argument whereas a Feeling type may well compromise the argument for the sake of harmony with the other person.

Feeling types tend to need more praise than Thinking types.

When out to dinner at a friend's house, the Feeling type will wash up just to be nice; the Thinking type may only wash up if there is a good reason.

Thinking types tend to be fair in their dealings with people; Feeling types, although they seldom like to admit it, can compromise fairness for what they believe in.

Thinking types will weigh things up whereas Feeling types tend to control the world from their beliefs and convictions.

Using these statements and other examples you can think of within the definitions described here, you can now plot your type on the scale below.

HOW DO I MAKE DECISIONS?

T|_____|_____|F
LOGIC   VALUES

Judging–Perceiving

Australian and US population J = 50%, P = 50%

How do you orient to the outer world?
This final scale describes the way you deal with the outer world and how you orient yourself in relation to it. This dimension refers back to the previous two scales. If you prefer the Judging side of this scale you will extravert your Thinking or Feeling function (whichever was your choice on the previous scale). If you choose the Perceptive side of the scale you will extravert your Sensing or Intuitive function (whichever was your choice on the second dimension discussed). Interestingly this Judging and Perceiving scale seems to define two very different types of people. Originally it was designed simply to help establish which was a person's dominant or most preferred function.

Judging
Those who choose a Judging attitude (either Thinking or Feeling) live in a planned, orderly way, wanting to regulate and control their external world.

When using your Judging function you are ordering your environment, being decisive, exacting, systematic and wanting to draw closure.

Organised
Decisive
Exacting
Systematic
Drawing closure

Perceiving

Those who have a preference for Perception when dealing with the outer world (either Sensing or Intuition) like to live in a spontaneous, relaxed and adaptable style.

When using Perception you are taking in information, keeping the options open and putting off making decisions.

Adaptable
Curious
Tolerant
Spontaneous
Avoiding conclusions

A number of examples may help to allow you to identify your preference on this scale:

Going on a holiday the Judging type will tend to have everything planned and booked in advance. The Perceiving type will want to be spontaneous and take things as they come.

18

Judging types like to get tasks accomplished, whereas Perceiving types rather like to enjoy the task.

Judging types can make decisions too quickly without enough data, whereas Perceiving types will tend to want to continue collecting data and put off making the decision.

Judging types need to achieve in life, whereas Perceiving types would rather enjoy life for itself.

Essentially Perceiving types prefer to stay open to experience, enjoying and trusting their ability to adapt to the moment. Judging types prefer to be structured and organised and to have things settled, wrapped up and finished.

Judging types tend to feel frustrated or annoyed when plans they have made are disrupted.

Using these statements and other examples that you can think of within these definitions you can now plot your type on the scale below.

HOW DO I ORIENT TO THE OUTER WORLD?

J|_____|_____|P
ORGANISED   ADAPTIVE

19

Summary of the Four Preferences

Your 'type' is the result of your own combination of preferences, which are stated for convenience in the form of four letters. You can take your four letters from your MBTI result and/or your analyses over the previous pages. Brief descriptions or profiles of each of the possible sixteen types are given on the following pages. If, when you read your type description, you feel comfortable with about 80 per cent of it, then this is most probably your 'type'. If the description does not feel comfortable and does not describe the type of person you are then it is most probably not your correct type. In this case you should return to the individual dimensions and choose another type profile, changing one or perhaps even two letters after re-examining the dimensions. If you have not completed an MBTI questionnaire at this point, you may find this exercise slightly more difficult. The MBTI is remarkably accurate in identifying a person's type.

Only you know your preferences and therefore only you can say what type you are.

Profiles of the Sixteen Types

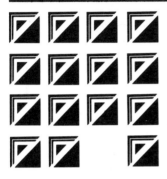

ENFJ

I am a charming, warm, enthusiastic and very highly gifted person. I often initiate new ideas and adventures, never doubting for a moment that people will want to do as I suggest.

My most specialised personality function, which I have developed for the outside world, is extraverted feeling. Reliance on this function gives me a very personal approach to life. I tend to judge everything in terms of my own values. I place a very high value on harmonious human contact. I am friendly, tactful and sympathetic. I can almost always express the right feeling at the right time.

My second best developed function is introvert intuition. As you get to know me you will realise that I have a quiet inner place in my personality which is good with theories and hunches. I am imaginative and I am always looking for possibilities in situations. The combination of my rich inner world of intuition and my outer world of feeling makes me an extremely creative and energetic person.

My type has a wide range of possibilities for occupations which offer success. We usually end up in jobs that deal with people. The media, ministry and the stage and screen are populated with successful people of my type. I make a superior therapist, a charismatic teacher, an excellent executive and a personalised sales person. I am attracted to almost any 'people to people' occupation where personal sustained contact is involved. This really capitalises on my personality. I have a tendency to talk a lot. Often I do not know what I'm going to say until I'm actually saying it. I take communication for granted. I believe that what I am saying will be understood and accepted. Just as I myself am accepting, so I assume that others will be equally accepting. I have a remarkable ability to relate to others with empathy. However, I have to watch that I don't become over-identified with others through picking up their burdens as though they were my own, for, in the process, I may risk my own sense of identity. In addition,

I find that on the one hand I have a natural flair for mimicking others, and on the other I can become over-extended emotionally without really knowing how it happened. I am socially adept and make an excellent companion and mate. I am also deeply devoted to my children. The danger here for my type is that I am so even tempered that I can often be victimised by my mate. I am always trying to please. I feel personally responsible for life at home, in fact in any environment in which I am involved, and I like things to flow harmoniously and smoothly. This dedication, however, often goes hand in hand with my dream of a perfect relationship. I long for the ideal. This can often result in a vague dissatisfaction with whatever impairs or obstructs relationships, mating as well as friendship ones.

I like to have things settled and organised. I prefer to plan both work and social engagements ahead. I tend to be absolutely reliable in honouring these commitments. I am very much at home in complex situations which require the juggling of much data, while at the same time I can handle people with absolute charm and concern. My type is usually popular wherever they go.

ENFP

I am an enthusiastic innovator, continually developing new ideas. I enjoy and am very able in dealing with people.

My most developed function is extraverted intuition, which leads me to be continually open to new possibilities and new ways of doing things. I have a thirst for imaginative and original projects that require lots of impulsive energy to carry out. I work in bursts and tend to start more things than I finish.

My second most developed function is that of introverted feeling, which leads me to an intense interest and concern for working with people. This introverted feeling function leads me into being quite an independent person, basing my decisions on personal priorities and values that I have chosen.

My type is often drawn to working in counselling or social work, where each new person presents a fresh problem to be solved, with fresh possibilities to be communicated. I would also make quite a good teacher, scientist, artist, or even advertising or sales person, as long as what I was selling was something I believed in. In fact, I can go into anything that interests me and do fairly well.

I am known for my optimism. I'm surprised when people or events don't turn out as anticipated. Often my confidence in the natural goodness of fate and human nature is a self-fulfilling prophecy!

Nothing occurs for me that does not have some meaning, and I tend to have an uncanny sense of the motives and thoughts of others. Naturalness and honesty are both very important to me. However, when I lose energy I tend to be my own worst critic, and can often end up being really hard on myself.

I enjoy intense emotional experiences but often have an uneasy sense of not being really present, as though a part of me was split off. I wonder sometimes if I'm in danger of losing touch with my real feelings, which I seem to possess in such a wide range and variety. I am certainly brilliantly perceptive, but I do have to be careful about being wrong in the conclusions I come to from my own perceptions. In other words, my mistakes tend to stem from my tendency to focus on things which agree with my own biases.

I am the typical sympathetic ear and natural rescuer. As a mate I tend to be charming, sympathetic and thoroughly non-conformist. I am not much bothered with daily routines, and I am usually seeking new outlets for my inspirations. This means I probably won't have a very tidy room! The mate of a typical ENFP can expect charming surprises, extravagant generosity, with occasional periods of stinginess. I am generally the one in charge of the home and I prefer it to be free of conflict. If I am left in charge of the financial resources we are likely to have extravagant luxuries in the home while necessities may be missing. I have little interest in detail, routine systems and regulations.

My life and work are thoroughly based on intuitions and beliefs.

INFJ ◪

I am quietly confident, somewhat individualistic. I have a deep intuition and a great depth of personality. In addition, I am very likeable. My type makes up only around 1 per cent of the general population.

Although people often don't see it, my most preferred function is introverted intuition, which makes me interested in possibilities, theories, hunches, and leads to my enjoyment of the past and the future rather than the present. I have an unusually deep, rich inner life, which gives me an uncanny ability to understand psychic phenomena better than most other types.

My second most preferred function, when facing the external world, is feeling. This is what most people meet me as. This leads me to

26

be apparently good and sympathetic with handling people and situations in the outside world. I can appear to be a very social personality, making sure things run smoothly and pleasantly at all times. In fact, this is more of an effort for me than people realise. My strong intuition makes it easy for me to intuit good and evil in others, although I can seldom say how I came to know. Subsequent events usually tend to bear out the truth of my intuitions. I am hard to get to know. People who have known me for years may find sides of me emerging which come as a surprise to them. Not that I am inconsistent—I am very consistent and value integrity. But I do tend to have a rather complex personality, which sometimes even puzzles me.

I like to please others and do my best in every situation. I prefer to agree with people rather than deal with the conflict of disagreement. I am capable of being a good student. I am creative, serious and often academic. I opt for occupations which involve interaction with people, but usually on a one-to-one basis. My type makes quite an outstanding individual counsellor, often being able to help people very deeply and meaningfully. I am highly sensitive in handling people and tend to work well in an organisational structure. I have a capacity for working at jobs which require solitude and concentration, but also do well when in contact with people, providing the human interaction is not superficial.

I need and want harmony in my house. I find any conflict, overt or covert, extremely destructive and uncomfortable. My friendship circle is usually fairly small, deep and long-standing. As a partner I am devoted and caring, but often need my own space. Incidentally, given the right environment I am probably the best cook of all the types—quite a gourmet!

As a parent I am fiercely devoted. I tend to bond very deeply with my children, leading often to an over-dependency that can be unhealthy for both myself and my child. At the same time I tend to be good friends with my children, while firm in discipline. I am concerned about the comfort, physical health and emotional well-being of both my mate and my children.

When you get to know me you will find I am both a deeply loyal and beautiful person.

INFP ▨

I am strongly independent, and yet have a deep wealth of feelings. My deepest feelings are seldom expressed, however, since my tenderness and passionate convictions are very reserved when with others. Inside I am feeling anything but distant.

My most preferred function is feeling, which is introverted and buried deeply in my inner world. I have chosen these feeling values without reference to the judgement of others and therefore I am extremely independent. I conduct most of my outward life with my intuitive function. This makes me open-minded, flexible and adaptable—until somebody crosses any one of my deeper feeling values, then I won't budge! In order to develop my intuitive feeling I have had to neglect my sensing and thinking functions, which tends to lead me to a distrust of people with a sensing/thinking preference.

I have a profound sense of honour, which comes from my internal feeling values. To understand me you really have to understand my cause, for I am willing to make the most profound sacrifices for someone or something in which I believe. One thing you may not notice about me immediately is the subtle, tragic motif running through my life—this is a minor key but important to understand. In many ways my life is rather a paradox. I am drawn on the one hand towards purity and unity, but on the other hand am always looking over my shoulder towards the sullied, the desecrated and the wild. I really do have my own value system, and it is difficult to understand where I'm coming from in my deep commitment.

At work I am most adaptable. I am generally aware of people and their feelings. I have been known to make errors of fact, but seldom errors of values. My type is found in all sorts of careers, although we have to work hard to prepare for a career in order to do well in it. My type is found in teaching, psychology and the world of computers. Incidentally, we also make outstanding novelists and character actors through our ability to efface our own personalities in the portrayal of a character.

My home is my castle. As a mate, I have a deep commitment. I like to live in harmony and may go to great lengths to avoid constant conflict. I am sensitive to the feelings of others and enjoy pleasing those for whom I care. As a parent, I am protective and devoted to my family. In day-to-day living I usually enjoy having decisions made on my behalf—unless my value system is violated! I then tend to dig my heels in and won't budge from my ideals. My life tends to go along gently for long periods, until an ideal is struck and violated—then I will resist and insist!

There are lots of my type in the counselling profession, but don't forget it's a lot of my type that end up going for counselling. I have a lot of difficulty making decisions, and dislike being put into boxes or being asked to obey formal rules, particularly rules laid out by organisations and institutions. I really am a most independent person. I enjoy life—especially the company of a few selected, trusted friends. To understand me you must understand that I have a rich inner life that guides and directs my outer life.

ENTJ ◪

I am a natural leader. I am sociable, outgoing, analytical and at ease with the world.

My most preferred function is extraverted thinking, which leads me to being logical, objective and systematic. My second most preferred function is intuition in the inner world, which leads me to be interested mainly in seeing the possibilities beyond what is present or obvious. Intuition heightens my interest and curiosity for new ideas.

Tolerance for theory, a taste for complex problems, insight, vision and concern for long-range possibilities are my strengths. I need to be very careful not to put down or avoid those who have a developed sensing feeling function, for this is exactly what I have neglected to develop in my life, in order to develop my strong intuitive thinking function.

I can be quite impersonal, while at the same time being sociable—I am good in the outside world of people and things, and yet can treat both people and things quite objectively.

I am the natural organiser; I am an organisation builder, and it is as if I cannot not lead. I usually find myself in command, and sometimes I am mystified as to how this happened. Anyway, I lead well, and with ease. In fact, I usually rise to positions of responsibility in whatever organisation I am within.

I tend to take charge of my home environment. When I am around there is little doubt who is in charge. However because my work is so important I tend to become increasingly absent from home. As a parent, I will tend to be in charge. The children will know what is expected of them—and will be expected to obey. People of my type are so often caught up in their careers that they have to make a real effort to be involved actively with their children and spouse.

It is important to me to have around someone with an active sensate function, to keep me from overlooking relevant facts and important details. I'm likely to be continually involved with new ideas, putting lots of them into practice. I don't like incompetence, and I like to know and do all things very well.

ENTP ◪

I am an enthusiastic innovator. I have lots of impulsive energy and initiative. I am fairly confident that I will be able to achieve almost anything I turn my hand to. My outer world is ruled by my extraverted intuitive function, which leads me to be imaginative, inspiring and ingenious. It also leads me into starting many things and often not finishing them off. My inner world (which people seldom see when they first meet me) is motivated by my introverted thinking function, which leads me into being quite logical, objective and organised. My intuitive and thinking functions together make me value competence, logic, knowledge, truth and perfection. They give me a mental ingenuity quite unknown to other types. In order to develop my personality type I have had to neglect both the sensing and feeling functions—these will be the challenge of my middle-life time.

I am an enthusiastic developer of ideas. One problem, however, is that I may take on too many new initiatives at the same time.

Although I am an analytical thinker, I am really quite slow to decide things. I like to have a lot of information before deciding and taking action. Of all types I am probably one of the best at using rules and regulations creatively to win. In fact, it's my type that changes jobs fairly regularly to avoid repetition and boredom. I'm confident in the value of most things that I do. I show a charming capacity to ignore what is traditionally done, or what the authorities say should be done. If somebody says to me 'It can't be done', my immediate response is to say 'I can do it'. My type can succeed in a variety of occupations as long as the work doesn't involve too much boredom or monotony. I tend to work in bursts of energy and move from one job to another with ease.

I am a fairly happy-go-lucky person at home. I am said to be over friendly. I certainly laugh easily, and often, and I am typically in good humour. Order and routine in daily life don't do anything for me. I would rather simply be involved in the daring adventure of living. Sometimes my type have been known to lead their families into physical and economic dangers. I like my mates to be competitive, and I enjoy living life to the full, using all the opportunities that come my way.

I am certainly not a critical person. In fact I

take people very much as they come. I need to be careful that I don't neglect the feeling side of my life and that I don't continually start things without bringing them to completion.

INTJ ◪

I am very individualistic, independent and self-confident. Underneath I may be quite vulnerable, but I am highly unlikely to tell you that. I tend to be logical, critical, decisive, determined and at times I am rather stubborn.

My most specialised function is introverted intuition, which makes me the great innovator in the field of ideas. I tend to trust my intuitive insights as to the relationships and meaning of things, regardless of established authority or popular beliefs. This inner world intuition leads me to question the meaning of most things and to work in bursts of energy.

My second most developed function is extraverted thinking. This is what you first meet in me; this is the logical, critical, somewhat cold face that I can often wear. My blunt and deliberate approach can often put people off, but when you get to know me you will find there's a wealth of feeling buried in my personality. In order to develop thinking I have neglected my feeling function; even more neglected is the sensate function, which may rear its head from time to time, leading me into such things as compulsive gluttony or compulsive buying.

I am the supreme pragmatist. I see reality as something that is quite arbitrary and made up, that it can be used as a tool—or ignored. Reality is really only there to help me refine my ideas, and in this sense my type is often called the most theoretical of all types. No idea is too far-fetched to be entertained.

As a mate, I want harmony and order in the home and in my relationship. I am the most independent of all types and could well be a perfectionist both at work and in the home. I am more comfortable in a working situation than a recreational one. I don't enjoy physical contact or touch, except with a chosen few. I tend to be dedicated and single minded in my devotion.

One of the hallmarks of my type as a parent is that I tend to be firm and consistent with my discipline, but rarely care to repeat directions given to children or others. In all this, I still have a strong need for my privacy and space.

One thing that stresses me highly is incompetence in myself or in others. I like to be able to do all things and to do them well. I am certainly the most misunderstood and rejected of all types; however if you give me another problem to solve I won't be concerned about this. If I am without a problem to solve I feel my vulnerability most fully.

It has been said of me that I need a staff to carry out my ideas—I tend to drive others almost as hard as I drive myself. I would make an efficient and good executive. My type usually rises to positions of responsibility, for we work long, hard and steady in our pursuit of goals, sparing neither time nor effort to get what we want. We are found in a variety of occupations; engineering and the computer world are high on the list. In fact, I am good in any job which requires the creation and application of technology to complex areas.

I am quiet, competitive and, as I said, a little vulnerable in my inner emotional life.

INTP ◪

I am a deep, creative thinker possessed with a desire to understand the universe. Only a few people really ever come to understand me. I am often taken either for granted or in the wrong way. I am seldom understood at my true level of competence. Some people see me as detached, objective, calculating and really little more than a social observer. However, they misunderstand me, as I am, in fact, deeply involved in the world around me.

My most preferred function is introverted thinking. I have specialised in using my introverted thinking to analyse the world, not to run it. I organise ideas and facts, not situations and people. Relying on thinking has made me logical, and objectively critical. I'm not likely to be convinced by anything that is not reasoned and logical.

My second best developed function, the face I give to people in the world, is extraverted intuition. It is very important for me that I develop this function, for indeed it is my tendency to remain continually in the inner world of thought. If I have developed my intuition I will see possibilities and theoretical value in things in the outside world. Remember that my type make up only a very small proportion of the population, about 1 per cent, so it is worth taking time to get to know me.

My obsession with analysis and seeking for natural law sometimes leads people of my type to careers in science, mathematics, research and the more complicated engineering areas. My type have been known to make fairly good scholars and teachers. I am, however, usually more interested in 'searching out' rather than 'reaching solutions and then putting them into practice'. Others can do this so much better than I can.

I am capable of working on complex problems; in fact, I can do so for very long periods of time. I cannot deny that I prize intelligence both in myself and in others. As a result of my need to amass ideas, principles and understanding, I may be thought of as a bit of a snob, or even an intellectual dabbler. Once I get caught up in a thought process it is as if that thought process had a will of its own. It is then that I need to persevere until the issue is understood in all its complexity.

In order to develop my intuition and thinking I have had to neglect my sensation and feeling functions. Neglecting sensation has made me rather forgetful, vague, and even a little absent-minded at times. Neglecting the feeling function makes it difficult for me to express my emotions verbally—in fact I am not very good in the feeling area at all. When my feelings do come to the surface, they are usually fairly primitive, child-like and rather overwhelming.

I am curious, adaptable, logical and analytical. I value honesty and the search for truth very highly—I am an idealist. Dig deeply with me, though, and you will meet a person of deep warmth, caring and affection.

ESTJ ▟

I am outgoing, organised, systematic, practical, factual and realistic. I am always responsible and punctual in doing my duty. I work to goals and look for logical approaches to everything I do.

My most preferred function is extraverted thinking, which makes me a logical, objective and organised type of person. My second most preferred function is sensation in the inner world, which makes me good with facts and details.

I am outstanding at organising orderly procedures, and rules and regulations. I like to see things done correctly. I tend to be impatient with those who do not carry out procedures with enough attention to those details. I am quite comfortable in evaluating others. I tend to judge how a person is doing in terms of standard operating procedures. I am, however, often accused of being a little too abrupt, blunt and deliberate. Unless I am in touch with my much lesser developed feeling side, I usually don't take any notice of this.

I am generally loyal to institutions, work and community. I make an excellent and faithful mate, as well as parent. I tend to solve problems by expertly applying and adapting my past experience. It is hard for me to be open to change. If I am married to a feeling or intuitive person, it will take a lot of courage for me to be open to my feeling side and the world of intuition. I am seldom willing to listen patiently to opposing views. I am especially vulnerable to this tendency when in a position of authority.

I am conservative in the best sense. I am so in tune with the established ways of behaving and doing things within institutions that I find it very difficult to understand those who want to change those institutions or established ways of doing things. I follow routines well at home and at work, tending to have a place for everything and wanting everything in its place. I'm neat and orderly, both at work and at play.

My type is often president of Rotary, Lions' Club or the St Vincent de Paul Society. I am committed to the traditions and usual way of doing things in society. I am attracted to jobs with a high level of order—shop floor manager, union executive, company director, garage owner—any position that can use my talent to organise, to decide and to put in order. Actually, it's my type that make up most of the bank managers!

I am relatively easy to get to know. I am dependable and consistent, and who I seem to be is probably who I am.

ESFJ

I radiate warmth and friendliness. I am outgoing, sociable and conservative in its richest sense.

My most preferred function is extraverted feeling. This reliance on feeling gives me a very personal approach to life, since feeling judges everything by a set of personal values. I place a very high value on harmonious human relations. Therefore I tend to be friendly, tactful and sympathetic. I can almost always say the right thing at the right time. My second most developed function is introvert sensate, which makes me practical, realistic, 'matter-of-fact' and concerned with the 'here and now'. In order to have developed sensing and feeling I have had to neglect intuition and thinking, hence I tend to distrust people who have developed an intuitive thinking capacity.

I am certainly energised by people. I do tend to idealise whatever, or whoever, I admire. Harmony is one key to understanding me.

I am very concerned with upholding and maintaining the established institutions such as the home, the school, the church and civic groups. At any social gathering I am usually there, both attending to the needs of others and trying to ensure that everybody is comfortable and involved. I tend to be rather hurt by coldness. I need to be appreciated for 'who I am' and even more importantly for 'what I do'.

I am usually attracted to work where I can serve people. I am good with selling, teaching, supervision, administration, coaching and, in general, people-to-people jobs. I am always loyal to my boss. In fact I tend to overwork, because of my deep sense of duty and service. As a mate I tend to have a set value system with clear 'shoulds' and 'should nots'. I expect my family to abide by these. I am conscientious, and a good worker around the house. As well, of course, I enjoy socialising and entertaining. I tend not to be rebellious, to be fairly deeply devoted to the traditional values of home and hearth, to respect my marriage vows, and to be the most sympathetic of all types of people.

I tend to be aware of, and agree with, the official decision-makers in society. Status is very important to me. I often depend on higher authority as the source of my opinions and attitudes. I am soft-hearted, sentimental and usually thoroughly enjoy birthdays and anniversaries, making any such event a delightful and important occasion. On the other hand, I am quite capable of getting very impatient with complications. I worry unduly over anticipated problems. As well, I have a lot of trouble responding to change. You can easily offset my stress by letting me know that I'm needed, and allow me to serve and to earn my daily wage.

ISTJ

I am decisive in practical affairs. I am dependable, practical and a matter-of-fact person.

My most preferred function is introverted sensation, which makes me very good with facts and details, leading to the enjoyment of the present moment. My second best developed function—the way I deal with the outside world—is extraverted thinking. This makes me appear, to the world, to be analytical, logical and decisive. I can have a blunt, deliberate approach to personal relationships, but the extra work needed to understand and appreciate others will be richly repaid, both in my work and in my private life. In order to develop sensing and thinking I have had to neglect both intuition and feeling. Therefore I may tend to distrust people with more highly developed intuitive feeling preferences.

My interest in thoroughness, due processes, details, justice and practical procedures leads me to occupations where these preferences are useful. For example, I would make an excellent bank examiner, auditor, accountant or tax examiner. I am not likely to take chances with my own or other people's money.

I have a dislike for and distrust of fanciness in speech, dress or home. I don't like things to be ostentatious. Neat, orderly, functional home and work environments are certainly my preference. My clothes tend to be practical and durable rather than in the 'latest style'. 'No nonsense', both in food and clothes, seems to characterise me. I am certainly not attracted to exotic foods, beverages or places.

As a partner I tend to be a pillar of strength. Just as my type honours business contracts, so do I honour my marriage contract. As a loyal and faithful mate I will take my responsibility to children and mate very seriously, giving lifelong commitment to this duty. The male of my type sees himself as the 'breadwinner' of the family, and as a consequence he is often quite patriarchal.

I am a steady and dependable partner. The female of my type may abandon the frivolous for the sensible. She may not always deepen her sensuality.

As a parent I tend to be consistent in handling children. The rules of the family will always be clear with me. Although I am outstandingly practical and sensible, my type often marries people who are in need of rescuing and reforming. The marriage relationship, unfortunately, develops into one of 'parent–child' rather than 'adult–adult'.

Normally, however, my type is a solid, outstanding mate, although sometimes it is said that 'ice, rather than blood, runs through my veins'. Despite this, I make up part of the thoroughly dependable backbone of our society. I am apt to be involved in community service organisations that transmit traditional values. I understand and appreciate the contributions these groups make in preserving the national heritage.

I tend to be a quiet, serious, persevering, patient and capable person. I highly value organisation and order, with clear roles and procedures. I prefer action to theory. Outwardly I show logical thinking, while inwardly I rely on detail and fact.

ISFJ

I am a particularly dependable personality who is sympathetic, tactful, kind and genuinely concerned and supportive to people—particularly to people in need. I am often attracted to fields where attention to detail is combined with a care for people.

My most preferred function is introverted sensation, which makes me very good with facts and details and leads to the enjoyment of the present. My second best developed function —the way I deal with the outside world—is extraverted feeling, which leads me to being a generally friendly, tactful and agreeable person. In order to have developed my sensate and feeling functions I have had to neglect my intuition and thinking functions. This may lead to my distrust of those with a more highly developed intuitive thinking preference.

I tend to be a steady person, valuing belonging, thriving on social stability and paying attention to detail. I carry a sense of history and tend to be somewhat old-fashioned at times. I am the least pleasure-loving of all types, and believe work is good and play must be earned. I use the old established ways of doing things and value doing them well. I prefer to do things by the book.

In fulfilling my desire to serve I may become overworked. I tend to repress by own needs in order to look after another's. This tendency can lead to migraine headaches and other stress-related illnesses.

I tend to be devoted and loyal to a boss. I identify with people rather than with institutions. I often feel personally responsible for seeing to it that people in an institution or business carry out established rules and routines. I am over-aware of status given by titles, offices and the values of society. I am aware of the value of material resources and do not like to see waste or misuse. To save or put something aside against an unpredictable future is very important to me.

I am devoted to my partner and family and am usually excellent as a homemaker. My home is most often kept well—both inside and out. As a parent I expect children to conform to the rules of society. I have a feeling of personal responsibility to see to it that these rules are honoured. While I seem to be super-dependable I may also be fascinated by and attracted to the irresponsible, the drunk and the glutton. Many of my type marry people in need. Initially this seems acceptable, only I find that I then proceed to conduct a rescue/rejection game without end. In consequence I suffer both greatly and unnecessarily. This and the worry over anticipated problems are dangers I should look out for. I also tend to be impatient with complications and have trouble responding to change.

I am frequently misunderstood and undervalued, as my contributions are often taken for granted. Despite this, however, the dependable, patient and invariable stability I offer makes me highly valued in the workplace and the home. I, along with the extravert of my type, are the feeling backbone of our society.

ESTP ▨

I am outgoing, charming and sometimes impulsive. I am a person of action, for when I'm around things begin to happen. I am superbly resourceful and enjoy an exciting environment, but at the same time I tend to be practical, pragmatic and look to do things in the easiest possible way.

My most preferred function is extraverted sensation, which leads me to experience a thorough enjoyment of the present moment. My second most developed function (which people seldom see) is my introverted thinking function, which makes me logical, analytical and somewhat interested in searching for truth and honesty.

Life is never dull around me. My attractive, friendly style has a theatrical flourish which makes even the most routine, mundane event exciting. I know the location of the best restaurants. Head waiters are likely to call me by name. I'm socially sophisticated, suave and a master manipulator of the external environment! I'm witty, clever and fun to be around, but I do find it difficult to understand when people say that I'm a bit overpowering.

I am fairly good at whatever I do in the workplace, although I often am unable to complete things that don't interest me. If my type is placed in a conservative job, they will tend to have an exciting and wild second life. For instance, as a bank clerk I would be likely to ride a 750cc motor bike to work, go mountain climbing on the weekend, or go wild animal hunting on my annual holidays. I just simply love action. If I'm put into a routine I'll become rigid and very hard to live with.

If my desire for excitement is not met constructively I may become tempted to do things that are destructive and antisocial. The 1970s movie *The Sting* picks up the actions and talents of my type of person: confidence trickery, counterfeiting, bad-cheque artistry, safe-cracking and swindling.

I tend to live in the immediate moment. As a partner I lend excitement—and unpredictability—to the relationship. I'm charming, smooth in social rituals, amusing and friendly. Although I seldom commit myself deeply to people, there is nothing too good for my mate and friends. I usually give generously and somewhat extravagantly.

I meet each day with a hearty appetite for the good things of life, searching out excitement, playing and seeking the thrill of courting 'Lady Luck' in one fashion or another. A theme of seeking excitement through taking risks runs clearly through my life.

ESFP ◪

I am a warm, optimistic, clever and realistic person. I am great fun to be with, very generous, and often the performer.

My most preferred way of being in the world is extraverted and sensate. This leads to my thoroughly enjoying the present moment. I notice, remember, and know what the facts are. Put quite simply, I enjoy life!

My inner world is ruled by my feeling function, and this backs my outer world sensation. I like to make decisions with my feeling-based value system rather than my more logical thinking system. This leads me to being quite tactful, sympathetic, interested in people, and generally at ease in handling human contacts. The development of my sensing and feeling function has been at the expense of my intuitive and thinking functions. This often leads me to distrust the more intuitive thinking type personality.

I tend to avoid being alone, seeking the company of others whenever possible. I crave excitement and create it wherever I am. I've been told that my joy of living is contagious and that I'm easy-going, witty and generally just good fun to be around. One of the dangers for me here is that I can easily be taken for granted—at times even taken for a ride. My

ESFP nature often leaves me open to be taken advantage of, and it is important for me to exercise more care. As a partner I'm exciting and good fun, if not somewhat unpredictable at times. I like my home to be unhassled and filled with people having a good time. I've been told I'm generous, but anyway what's mine you're welcome to have. I'm happy to give assistance to anyone without expectation of a return. I guess I expect everybody else to be the same. Pleasure and fun are what it's all about anyway, so why not let's enjoy them together.

I tend to avoid anxiety, and when there's sickness or trouble I find it difficult to stay around. I may become impatient and want to absent myself.

On the work scene I have good common sense. I enjoy jobs with plenty of activity. I am quite outstanding in public relations and working with people. My type is seldom interested in school or scholastic pursuits. I only want knowledge for its immediate use. I am often a good sales person. I tend to gravitate towards selling tangible things in business. I am good at working with people in crisis. My enjoyment of entertaining people often draws my type to the performing arts, since we thrive on the excitement of being in the limelight.

If you want to have a good evening out, going

to all the best places in town, I am bound to be the person for you. I am easy-going, tactful, charming, sophisticated, impulsive and thoroughly social. I enjoy direct experience, and my personal beliefs rule my life style.

ISTP ▢

I am skilful, realistic and relatively unemotional. I value action, impact, spontaneity and doing things my own way in a practical fashion.

My most preferred function is introverted thinking, which tends to make me logical, impersonal, objectively critical and good with organising ideas and facts, but no so good with organising situations and people.

My second most developed function is extraverted sensate. This leads me to an intense enjoyment of the present moment. In my social life this explains my impulsive search for involvement in the here and now. I enjoy fun, play and daring activities. My type is said to be patient, accurate, good with their hands, fond of sports and the outdoors. I have a gift for fun!

Although I don't like to show off who I am (and certainly don't like to be put in a box!) my nature is most easily seen in my mastery of tools—tools of any kind, from the microscopic drill to the supersonic jet. You will often find my type in the so-called unskilled labour force—climbing tall buildings, driving earth movers, using tools of any kind; driving, steering, operating tools indicates my presence. It is only other types who call us unskilled, but unfortunately they worked out the education system we tended not to fit into! The brilliant artist of our type is personified in Michaelangelo or Leonardo da Vinci—we're a very talented type, but more keen on working with our tools on personal impulse than on being scheduled or organised. If an externally-imposed schedule coincides with my impulse, fine—if not, so much the worse for the schedule!

If people of my type happen to be in more regimented professions, they probably have another life on the side. The specialist doctor is a rock climber on the weekends or rides a motorcycle to the airport. I like to play on impulse, taking off at any time just because I feel like it.

Paul Newman is another example of my type. On the one hand he is a fine actor, an intense thinker, on the other a proficient and daring racing car driver.

I am obviously skilled with machines and technology. I can exercise clear leadership in these areas. Despite my friendliness, individualism and love of freedom, I am quite capable of being a great leader. However I must be in the front, sword in hand as it were, leading the charge. My supreme realism, timing and sense of the exact moment allow me to fully exploit the resources of any situation. This explains my obvious interest and talent in sports.

My type is usually very intelligent, although, as I have said, the education system has not been designed for us. I dislike 'shoulds', and learn best through activity—give me a tool or machine-centred curriculum and watch my speed.

I am usually easy-going and well intentioned, as long as you don't lay any obligations, duties or confining promises on me. I am un-complicated in my desires, and tend to be trusting, open and generous.

ISFP ▨

I like to live in the here and now. I have a deep, personal warmth. I am sympathetic, friendly and practical. I particularly do not like to be put into a box or categorised in any way. I value freedom and action. I like to do things to learn them rather than to learn things in theory.

My favourite and most developed function is introverted feeling. This gives me a wealth of warmth and enthusiasm. I tend to judge every-thing against my own personal values. Loyalties and ideals govern my life, but my deepest feelings are seldom expressed. I tend to wear a mask of quiet reserve.

The way I deal with the world is with my extraverted sensate function, which leads me to enjoy the present moment—the here and now. This allows me to be an open-minded, flexible and adaptable type of person. I have times of thoroughly enjoyable excitement and doing daring things.

I show my warmth and commitment to people more by the things I do than the words I say. I am compassionate towards anything helpless. I work well at any job requiring devotion. People call me gentle, considerate and retiring; however, I feel I am only an ordinary sort of person. I am in touch with the very real—and this is what I feel life is all about!

I found it hard to make it through school. I didn't really like to be told to sit in a row to learn by listening. I have the intelligence of the artisan (no less real than the intelligence of the other types, and yet not as valued by the education system). Beethoven, Rembrandt and other great artists were of my type. I am likely to be found in jobs requiring artistic talent. I enjoy practical activities. I like to be in touch with practical issues. I would prefer, for ex-ample, to act in an organisation rather than being caught up in it. Deep down, anyway, I do not believe in the rules of any institution. I have my own value system. Realistically, I want to do my own thing. People of my type often work in support organisations, such as the Salvation Army and St Vincent de Paul—helping people in need. However, I am extremely reluctant to tell anybody that I am doing it. My action is my commitment.

I am committed as a mate. Try not to tie me down. I am a free spirit with a special kind of intelligence that people usually don't understand. I enjoy children intensely. I will probably be more devoted than most to mate and family. It is important that nobody tries to constrain me, delay me or make me fit into any rigid system.

I am open, flexible and pragmatic. Even though my deeper feelings are seldom shown, I do have a deep strain of caring running throughout my life.

Portraits of the Four Temperaments

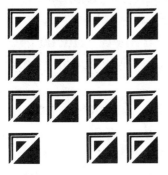

To this point in analysing types you will probably be able to identify your own personality type and perhaps that of one or two other people. In this section of the handbook we will generalise type even further and speak of only four fundamental types or temperaments. This exercise will help to bridge your understanding of the other types and particularly those that are distinctly different from your own.

Each of the four types of temperaments that follow is based on two of the letters from the type formula: NF, NT, SJ and SP. For the first two we use the two middle letters, and for the last two we use the first of the two middle letters and the last letter. This is simply a way of breaking up type. You will notice in your reading that other authors use other methods of breaking up type such as: NF, NT, SF and ST or EJ, IJ, EP and IP; each way has its value. The temperament theory we are using here has its roots in the basic temperament types of Greek mythology.

The following pages outline the values, skills, weaknesses and stress responses of each of the four temperament styles. Compare your chosen type with this further generalisation. Again, all of us do things from all four of these styles—but one will tend to reflect your preference.

NF	SJ
ENFJ	ESTJ
ENFP	ESFJ
INFJ	ISTJ
INFP	ISFJ
NT	SP
ENTJ	ESTP
ENTP	ESFP
INTJ	ISTP
INTP	ISFP

NF: ENFJ ENFP INFJ INFP

The Catalyst

I value authenticity, integrity and harmony and

my life is partly summed up as a search for meaning.

To determine my own destiny is a high priority; I thrive on autonomy and self-determination. I hunger for self-actualisation—there must not be a facade, or mask, or sham or pretence in living. I am a high-energy person for things I believe in—it is often said I can sell anything I believe in, especially my own value system.

My type make up only 13 per cent of the general population: we are rare but we tend to flock together. You will find us where there is a cause, but it must be a cause of lasting and deep significance. The majority of personal counsellors, ministers, social workers and other helping professionals are NFs. We are deeply attuned to people and naturally empathetic. The most appropriate jobs for us are those where we can make a unique contribution.

As a manager I focus on the growth needs of an organisation. I tend to make decisions by participation and I firmly believe that people's potential is an organisation's strength— motivated workers equal high productivity.

My weaknesses include the tendency to over-involvement, the difficulty I have with structures and authority. As a manager I must avoid playing favourites, putting others' needs and priorities before my own, and being too anxious to please. I must also be careful not to 'sweep problems under the carpet'.

My main stress comes when I experience a loss of integrity or identity, severe guilt or when I am radically over-extended. To counteract that stress I need time alone and lots of strokes!

NT: ENTJ ENTP INTJ INTP
The Visionary Builder

I value competence, logic, knowledge, truth and perfection, and my search is to be able to do everything I put my hand to, well.

I regard principles highly. I am good with conceptual things and I can usually see patterns in complexity. Intellectual ingenuity, pioneering and predicting, sophisticated understanding of systems and problem solving are all skills of mine.

My type make up only 12 per cent of the general population. We need to work in jobs that use our skills, learning is a twenty-four-hour preoccupation, we have almost a passion for knowing. We excel in technology, science, mathematics, philosophy, engineering, architecture—in fact anything complicated and exacting. However we tend not to do things that we feel incompetent in. Whatever I do I do competently—of course!

As a manager I tend to focus on the mission and systems of the organisation. I like planned approaches to change, logic and common sense and I am consistently good at generating ideas.

I am loath to admit I have any weaknesses—and this may be my greatest weakness! I hate incompetence—if I have given instructions once then that should be enough—'I suffer fools very badly!' I have to watch to maintain my interest after the design phase and I must learn to be more patient with human concerns.

Don't tell anybody, but I actually have one area of massive incompetence—I hide it well, but it's there. For my type it is often the personal area, but it can be any area—it tends to balance me and I shouldn't spend so much energy denying it.

I'm stressed by incompetence of course—not being able to know and do all things well, and I always seem to have escalating standards for myself—and others. I can, however, counteract that stress by having a problem to solve.

SJ: ESTJ ESFJ ISTJ ISFJ
The Stabiliser

I value the following:

1. social stability
2. loyalty
3. security

4. industry
5. right order
6. belonging

I am cautious, careful, usually steady paced and certainly reliable. If rules have been made one should keep them—due process is important to me.

My skills include:
1. attention to detail
2. being dependable
3. stabilisation
4. acccuracy of work
5. common sense
6. keeping deadlines

Some say I am the 'salt of the earth', but I'm not one for fancy expressions (or any of this airy fairy psychology stuff usually). I am practical and I need to see results!

My type makes up 40 per cent of the general population. We run and dominate the armed services, the police force, financial institutions, government and law-making bodies, and we regard most long-standing institutions of society with respect. As a manager I need to know the hierarchy of the organisation. I'm good at establishing policies, rules and schedules; I need to see a product that meets the set standards and I like the organisation to run on solid facts.

Given my type's dedication to established

social norms and institutions it is no wonder you will find us in business, in service occupations, in secretarial and administration work, in accounting, the law, in the public service and in teaching. I believe in an 'honest day's pay for an honest day's work'.

One weakness I have is that I do tend to worry over anticipated problems. I see no value in change for its own sake and I am good when it comes back to the consolidation and stabilisation phase again.

I am stressed by rejection and exclusion, others not employing standard operating procedures and ignored deadlines. You can help relieve my stress by letting me know I am needed.

SP: ESTP ESFP ISTP ISFP
The Negotiator Trouble-Shooter

I value freedom, fun, change, flexibility, action and spontaneity. Bottom line: I must be free. I will not be tied down, or confined, or obligated. 'Enjoy today for tomorrow never comes!' I enjoy impulse, I have acute observation skills, I'm open-minded, fairly tolerant and certainly realistic.

Give me a crisis and you see me at my best—I get bored with the status quo and goals are secondary to me. I guess I'm fairly generous—but don't expect me to tell you that. I'd rather simply do good things for people, forget the praise.

The action-hunters, performers, the mercenary soldier, the gun-slinger of the 'wild west', the stunt person, the racing car driver, the negotiator or IR person—these are all likely to be SPs. Then again you may find my type in a 'normal' job—but watch me when I play!

As a manager I concentrate on the expedient needs of the organisation. I tend to be crisis stimulated. I have a good sense of timing, cope well with change, and usually don't mind taking risks.

My weaknesses include being impatient with theories and abstractions (actually I don't see that as a weakness!), shooting from the hip (but that's fun because you never know what might happen), and a tendency to ignore the past and its implications for the future. You can stress me by constraining, restricting, categorising or delaying me. I counteract these stress situations with action to restore my impulse.

Essentially I am practical, flexible and pragmatic. Now let's get back to life ...

The Four Functions of Each Type

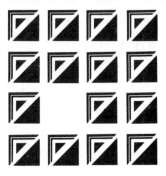

Each of us uses all four functions, but to different degrees. Two of the four functions will tend to be conscious and two unconscious.

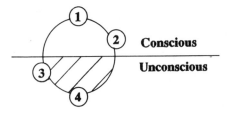

Each person has a preferred Perceiving function, either Sensation or Intuition, and a preferred Judging function, either Thinking or Feeling. You know which are your preferences from the two middle letters of your type formula. One of these two letters will be the Dominant function and the other the Auxiliary function.

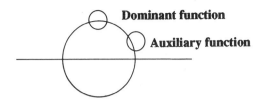

Dominant function

Auxiliary function

The way we establish which of the two functions is Dominant and which is Auxiliary is by going to the first and last letter of the type formula.

The first letter, E or I, should be placed beside the No.1 or Dominant function. You then need to place the other, E if you are I or I if you are E, in the No.2 or Auxiliary function.

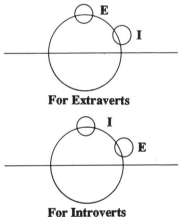

E

I

For Extraverts

I

E

For Introverts

Now we go to the last letter. This is going to tell us which function we Extravert (this is simply the way the questionnaire is constructed). If your formula finishes with J then your T or F (whichever is in your formula) goes beside your ·E. If your type formula finishes with P then your S or N (whichever is in your formula) goes beside your E. The other letter goes beside the remaining function.

The following table has the Dominant function of each type underlined.

The Dominant Process of Each Type

I—J	I**S**TJ	I**S**FJ	I**N**FJ	I**N**TJ
I—P	IS**T**P	IS**F**P	IN**F**P	IN**T**P
E—P	E**S**TP	E**S**FP	E**N**FP	E**N**TP
E—J	ES**T**J	ES**F**J	EN**F**J	EN**T**J

The Tertiary and Inferior functions are opposite to the Dominant and Auxiliary functions as shown below.

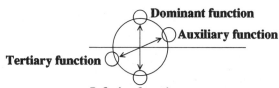

Following is the circle diagram noting Dominant, Auxiliary, Tertiary and Inferior functions for each of the sixteen types.

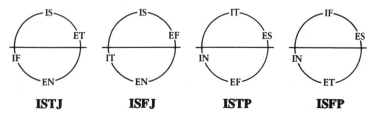

68

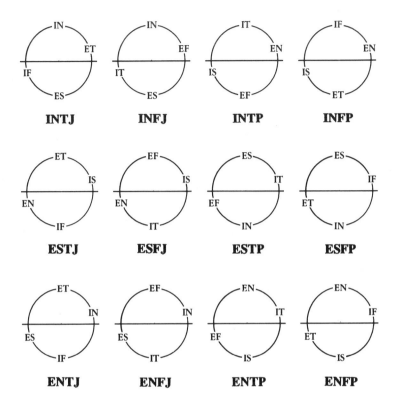

We can each identify, then, at least theoretically, which are our Dominant, Auxiliary, Tertiary and Inferior functions. We in fact have better use and superior control of the Dominant function. The Auxiliary function, however, is very important to balance the strength of that Dominant function. We need this balance. Jung in his *Psychological Types* outlined the psychotic and neurotic tendencies of type when people use only their Dominant function. Basically the Extravert becomes increasingly extraverted and moves towards hysteria, the Introvert becomes increasingly withdrawn, having no relation to objective reality.

We need to use all four of our functions and it is particularly important to have the balance of our Auxiliary function.

Finally a note on the Inferior function. It is the opposite to our Dominant or most preferred function. We have little control of this part of our psychology, we often project it onto others, and it is usually our greatest area of vulnerability. It is primitive, childish and often tyrannical.

The Inferior function is often the 'blind spot' in our nature. We need to look at this part of ourselves and not run from it. Basic to Jungian psychology is that the unconscious can and will come in to enlarge consciousness and bring forth new attitudes.

Management Uses of the MBTI

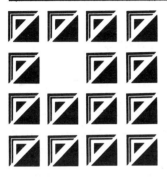

The MBTI is now recognised as one of the most respected professional testing instruments in psychology. It has gained wide acceptance for its corporate applications and has been thoroughly researched and validated as a measure of personality difference. It is a very valuable tool in assisting individuals and groups within any industry to attain improved performance and professional growth through greater understanding of their personal styles and inherent attitudes.

The predictive information about behaviour on the job yielded by the MBTI, along with the quite precise distinctions between the types, is one of its clearest assets in the management and organisation development fields. Experience in applying such a psychologically based scientific method in selection, for example, can vastly improve management's ability to make a successful job–person match. That same knowledge can also give managers specific information for day-to-day coaching as well as for periodic employee performance appraisals and feedback. Additionally, the model remains dynamic, which means that people are seen to be able to change, perhaps not fundamentally but certainly in their ability to use less preferred modes of behaviour. The MBTI gives individuals language to speak of their strengths and preferences and it gives an organisation a philosophy of effective human resource management.

Management and Organisational Applications

Type theory is used extensively in management development to help managers understand their natural strengths and areas of potential for development. It provides an effective context for examining one's leadership style, communication style, and how one approaches planning and problem solving. It is also useful for examining those tasks preferred by managers, the areas of support they most need from others, the kinds of expectations they hold for performance, and the style they use for giving feedback and appreciating the contributions of others.

A manager can apply type theory in a real, practical sense throughout various aspects of the human resource management process. Some practical examples of the application of type theory are:

- Organisational development training programmes
- Team building
- Creative problem solving
- Interpersonal communications
- Role negotiation
- Motivation methods and techniques
- Conflict resolution
- Delegation skills
- Stress management
- On-the-job and classroom training
- Marketing and sales development
- Company evaluation and analysis
- Performance appraisal and reward systems
- Job description and/or redesign
- Career path counselling

- Staff selection and external recruitment
- Internal promotion
- Interviewing, coaching and counselling

The MBTI is a powerful management, training and diagnostic tool, assisting management in the diagnosis of existing and potential individual and organisational performance problems, and also providing a firm basis for correction and improvement. Numerous companies, particularly in the United States, Europe and Japan, have now used the MBTI with excellent and quantified results. One particular Japanese multinational company tested some half-million employees and showed a measured increase in productivity and job satisfaction, a decrease in industrial accidents and absenteeism, and an overall improvement in profitability.

In interactions between supervisors and subordinates, or among peers, the MBTI can be a useful tool for improving communications, resolving conflicts, and developing a tolerance and appreciation for each other's work style. Type helps people understand how differences that have previously seemed irritating and obstructive become amusing, interesting and a source of strength in a relationship. It can provide a powerful and productive team-building intervention.

The MBTI provides a useful context for

facilitating effective interactions in work teams and increases the awareness of team members around process issues. It can be used in structuring group meetings so as to capitalise on the strengths of the group, avoid potential weaknesses and maximise the contributions of each member. The use of type will also support individual development as the members learn from each other's skills. Type can also be used to ensure diversity in the selection of teams or task forces, and to facilitate the effective application of their differences to the problem-solving process.

It is stressed that the real practical advantage of the MBTI is that it does not produce negative results about a participant. The MBTI is beneficial in the development of individuals and organisational climates simply because it recognises skills and abilities and potential for development, which differ according to the type of the individual.

MBTI Test Materials and Accreditation Programs

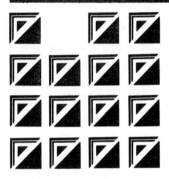

MBTI test materials are available to psychologists and suitably qualified professionals in Australia from the Australian Council for Educational Research, PO Box 210, Hawthorn, Victoria 3122, and in the United States from Consulting Psychologists Press or the Centre for the Applications of Psychological Type.

Further information on the Australian norms and data base, further publications and the Australian MBTI Accreditation Training Programs can be obtained from the author, G.P.O. Box 2728, Brisbane, Queensland 4001.

MBTI is a registered trade mark of Consulting Psychologists Press Inc., 577 College Av., Palo Alto, Ca. 94306, USA.

Other helpful titles from Collins Dove

LET A VIKING DO IT
Peter Malone

In this attractive and amusing book, Peter Malone harnesses the wit of Hagar the Horrible cartoons to the insights of Myers-Briggs psychology.

The author first explains features of the 16 personality types—or tendencies—classified by the Myers-Briggs Type Indicator. The Indicator, by now well-known in counselling and management circles, was developed in the light of Carl Jung's work.

Though others have offered commentary on the Myers-Briggs scheme in words, until now no one had seen the possibilities of using cartoons. Here Hagar and Helga and their family not only exemplify the theory, but make it all too possible to recognise one's own personality type—and those of others, too.

These new understandings and possibilities for better communication will be found valuable by expert and general reader alike. The author proves once more that the best teaching always includes humour and an element of entertainment—and that these need not trivialise the topic at hand.

56 pp. 245 x 170 mm PB; ISBN 0 85924 711 2

THE HERO JOURNEY IN DREAMS
Joan Dalby Clift & Wallace B. Clift

According to the Talmud, dreams left uninterpreted are like letters left unopened. In their previous book, *Symbols of Transformation in Dreams*, which was hailed by John Sanford as 'one of the best on the subject', The Clifts showed how dreams can affect our decisions and transform our lives.

In their latest book, the Clifts turn to the myth of the hero and to the question of the meaning of the heroic quest. Starting from the notion that hero stories describe a growth in consciousness and correspond to life's experiences, the Clifts go further to show how dreams, in responding to the life being led by the dreamer, resonate with the motifs of the hero journey. Such dreams offer ordinary individuals clues to realising their full purpose in life.

The balance of the book, with its scores of illustrative dreams and abundance of clues and principles for interpretation, is an informed and informal guide to the symbols of transformation in our dreams that point to various stages and aspects of the hero journey. Ultimately, the book shows how the need for heroism is never outgrown, only deepened and expanded.

228 pp. 216 x 140 mm PB; ISBN 0 85924 749 X

JUNG AND CHRISTIANITY
Jean Dalby Clift & Wallace B. Clift

Jung himself felt that he had been chosen by God for a unique contribution to the world. He felt also that he had a unique contribution to make to the church. Today his message is perhaps more relevant than ever. Clift's book is just the book we have been waiting for.

Jung's world view is extremely strange and difficult to grasp. Few readers are in a position to make a judgement on much of his thought as he draws on so many divergent cultural traditions: mythology, the Bible, gnosticism, alchemy, eastern philosophy and religion, mediaeval mysticism, Christian theology, modern psychoanalysis, modern science, physics and art and especially his own vast clinical experience.

Clift does a great service in presenting Jung's thought clearly and simply outlining the contributions and challenges he presents to the church and analysing these in the light of Christian tradition and in relation to our current dilemmas and possible future directions.

186 pp. 216 x 140 mm PB; ISBN 0 85924 243 9

EDUCATING PSYCHE : EMOTION,
IMAGINATION AND THE UNCONSCIOUS IN
LEARNING
Bernard Neville

This is a book about good teaching.

In spite of a lot of talk about change, what teachers do in
classrooms today does not differ very much from what
they were doing twenty, fifty or even a hundred years
ago. Those who try to do things differently are likely to
be told that what they are doing is not 'real teaching', or
that they are a threat to the good order of the school. Yet
over the past hundred years we have learned a great deal
about the mind/brain and how it functions, and a lot of
what we have learned has clear implications for what
teachers ought to be doing if they want to be effective and
successful in their task.

This book is about the psyche, the whole mind, and calls
on what we have learned from Jung, Freud, Coué,
Assagioli, Moreno, Erickson and other students of the
mind to tell us how we might go about a fully human
education. It is also about Psyche, the goddess, and
explores her myth and the myths of other gods as images
of the 'other side' of education, the side neglected by
teachers who think only that teaching means 'telling them
things'.

It is a book about indirect learning, suggestion, trance,
psychodrama, relaxation, autogenics, bio-feedback,
visualisation, intuition, mind-control, meditation, not as
entertainments or as substitutes for 'real-teaching' but as
approaches and techniques which can contribute to
teaching and learning.

400 pp. 216 x 140 mm PB; ISBN 0 85924 777 5

SYMBOLS OF TRANSFORMATION IN DREAMS
Jean Dalby Clift & Wallace B. Clift

This is a very special book—an innovative guide to understanding the messages which dreams bring us from the spiritual reality that prods us towards wholeness and fellowship with itself.

The authors speak to the centre and heart of human life—transformation—with eloquence and clarity. They include many illustrative dreams along with interpretations; these will help both the beginner and the professional in understanding their own dreams. They deal in depth with some of the most common dream symbols: snakes, death, the trickster, shadow figures and the many images by which the holy is revealed in our dreams.

I was personally touched by this book and could hardly put it down until I finished it. *Symbols of Transformation in Dreams* is thoughtful, innovative, practical and personal.'
Morton T. Kelsey

160 pp. 216 x 140 mm PB; ISBN 0 89524 748 1